Snc

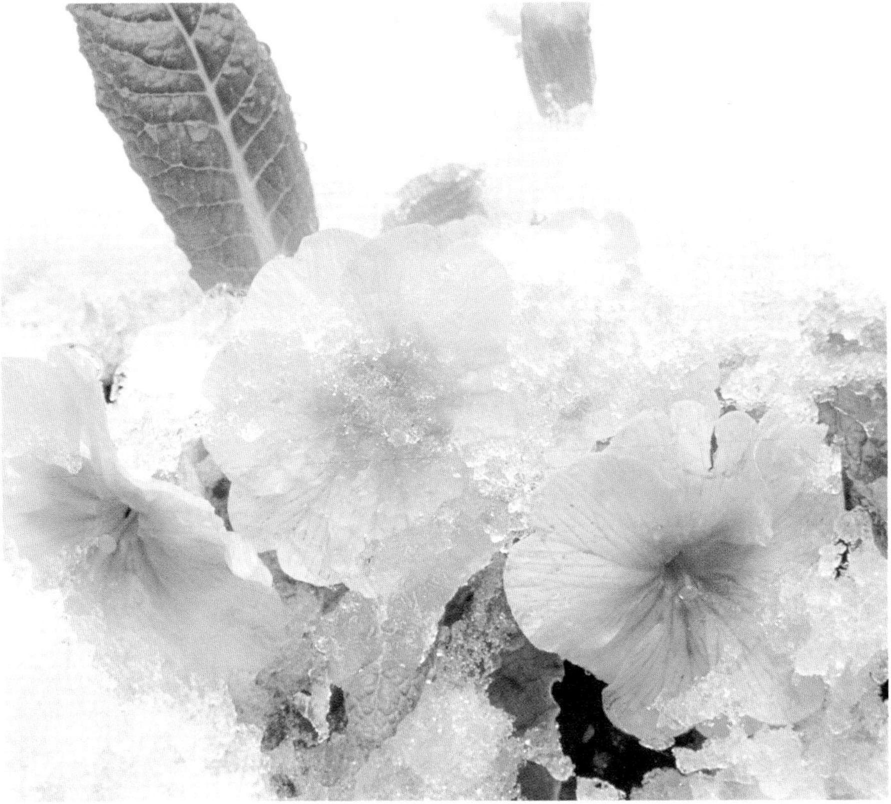

Lisa Trumbauer

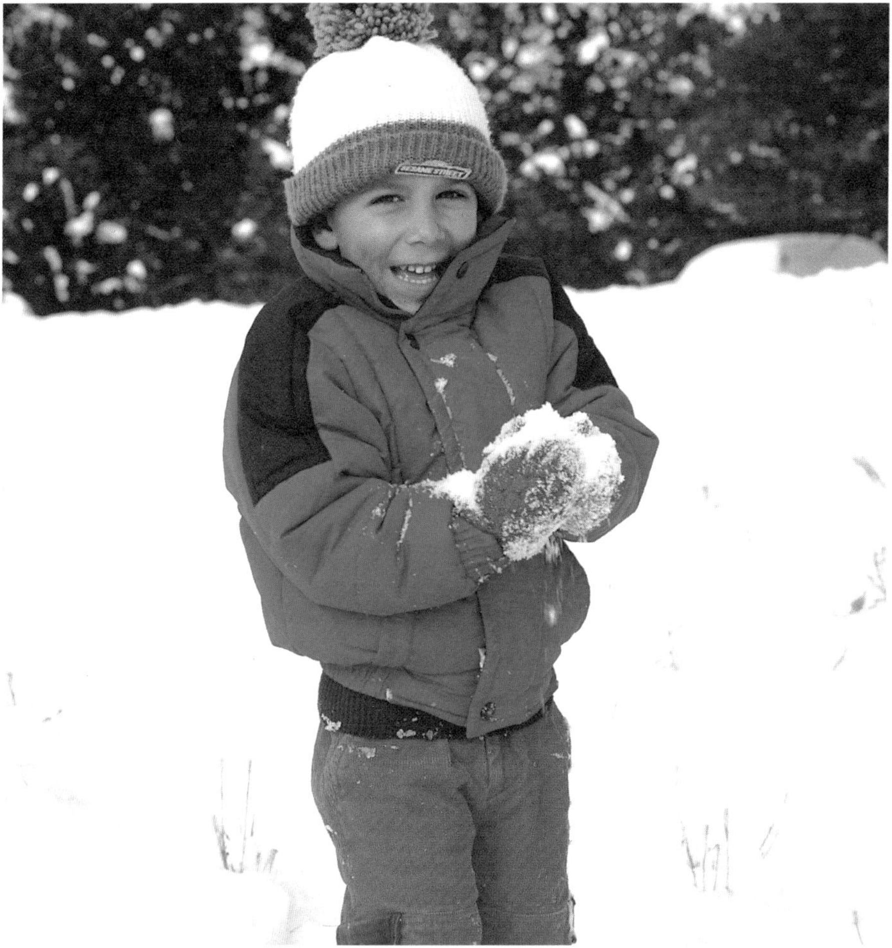

Snow on my hands.

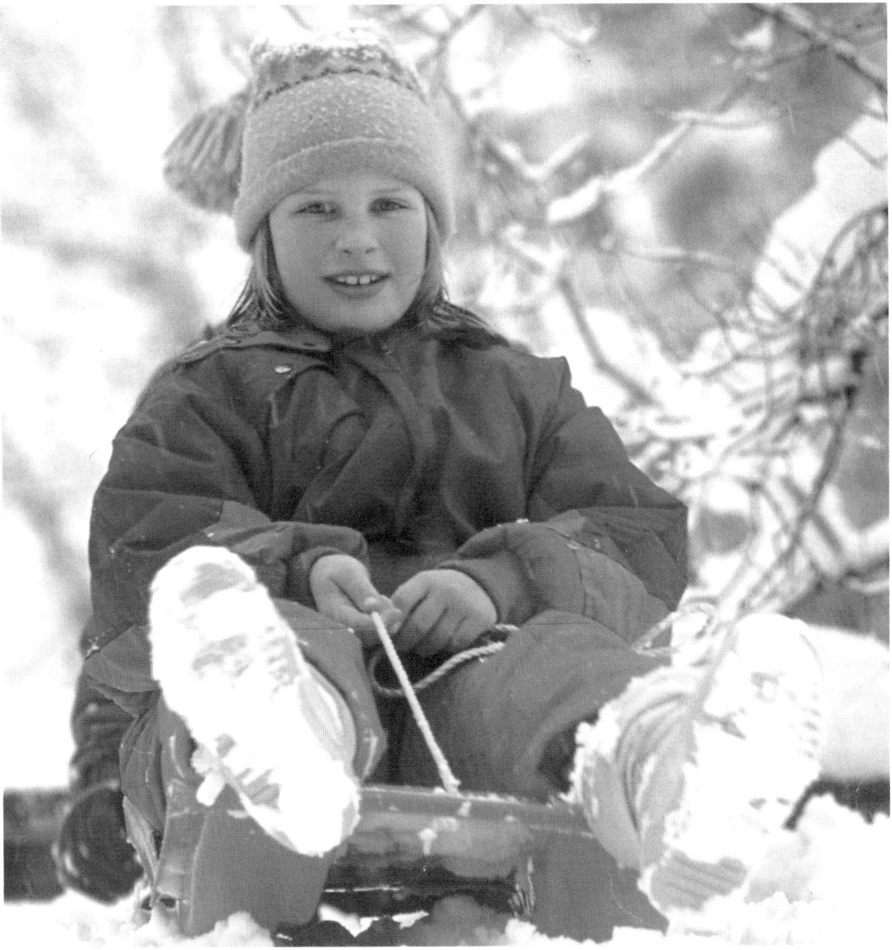

Snow on my feet.

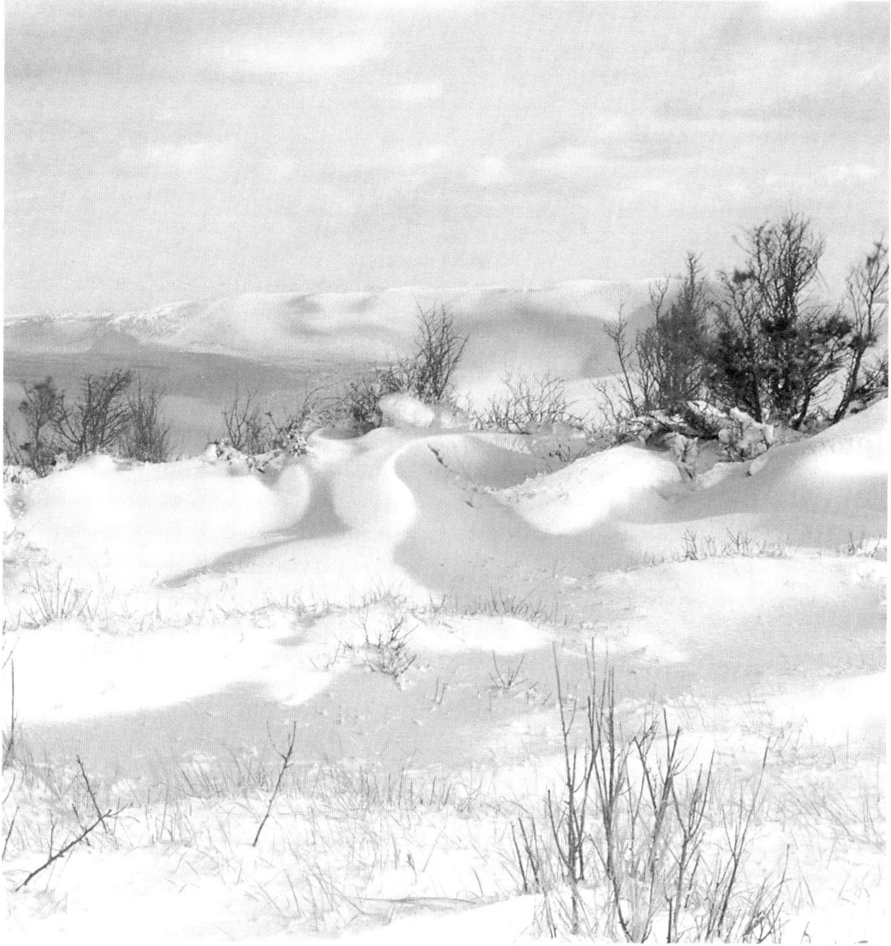

Snow on the sand.

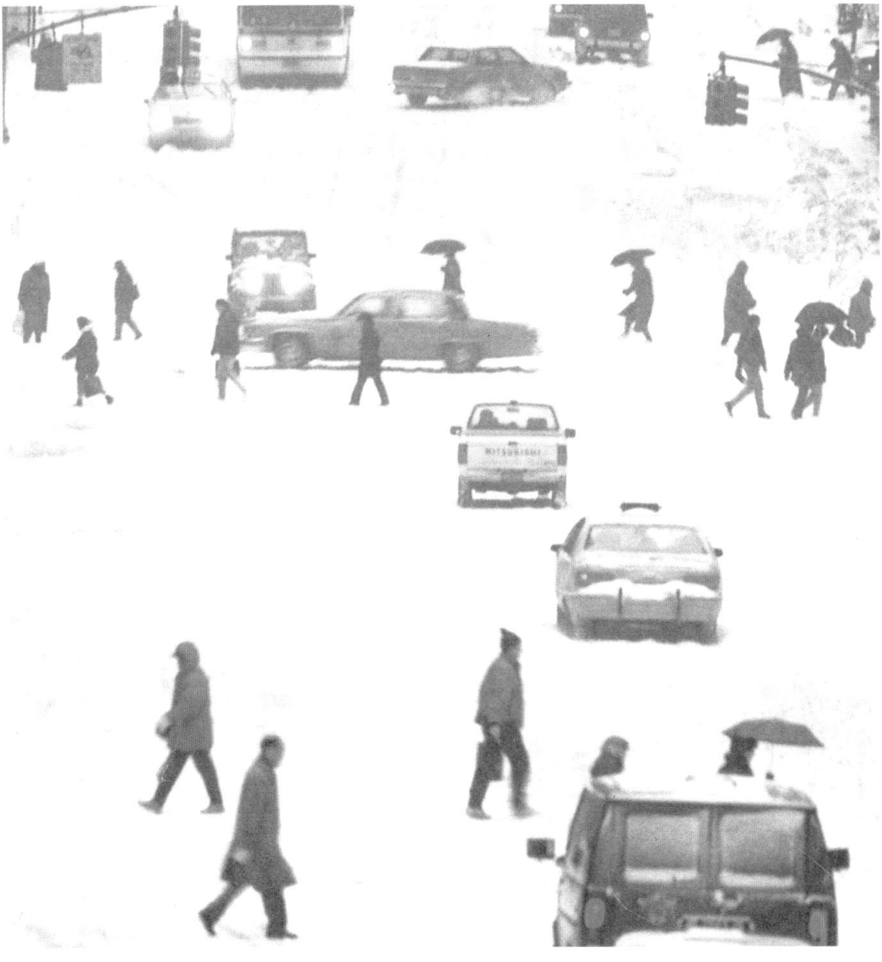

Snow on the street.

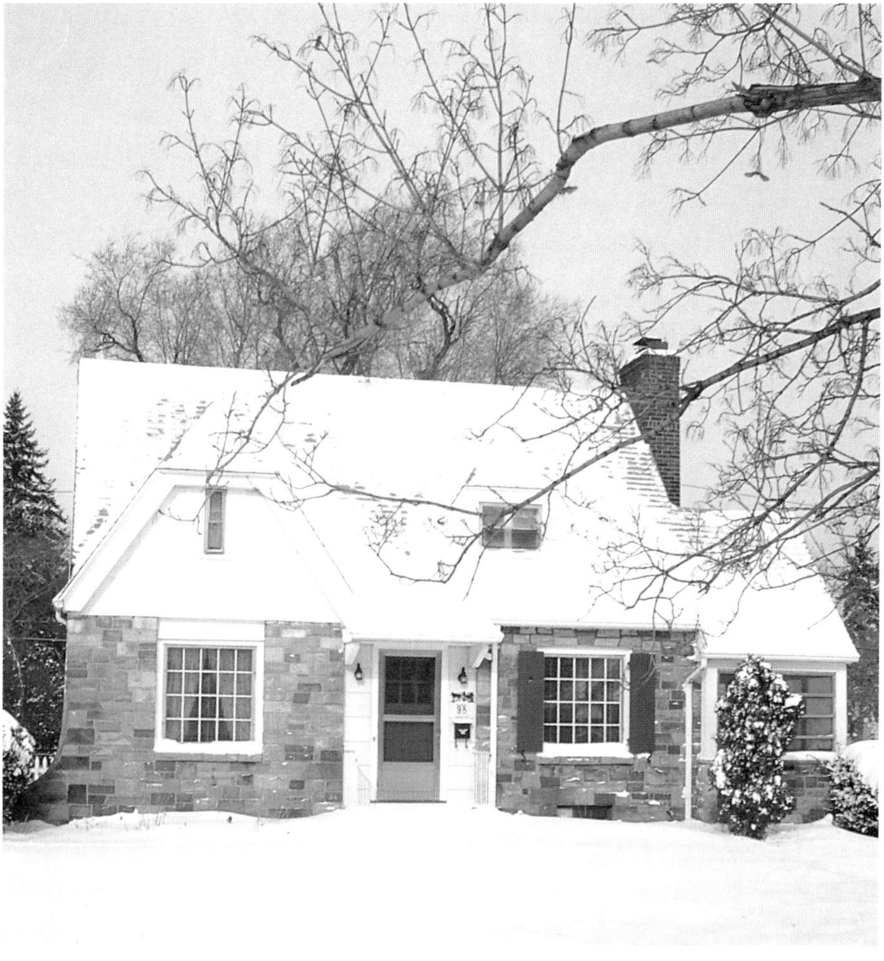

Snow on the house.

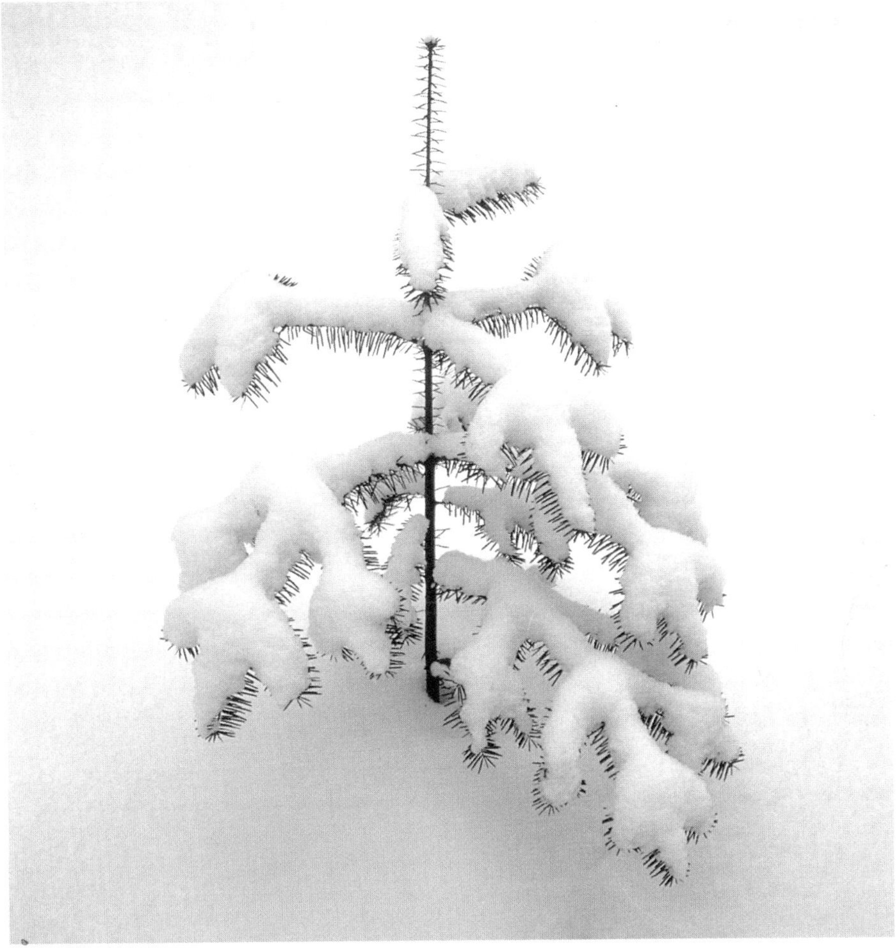

Snow on the tree.

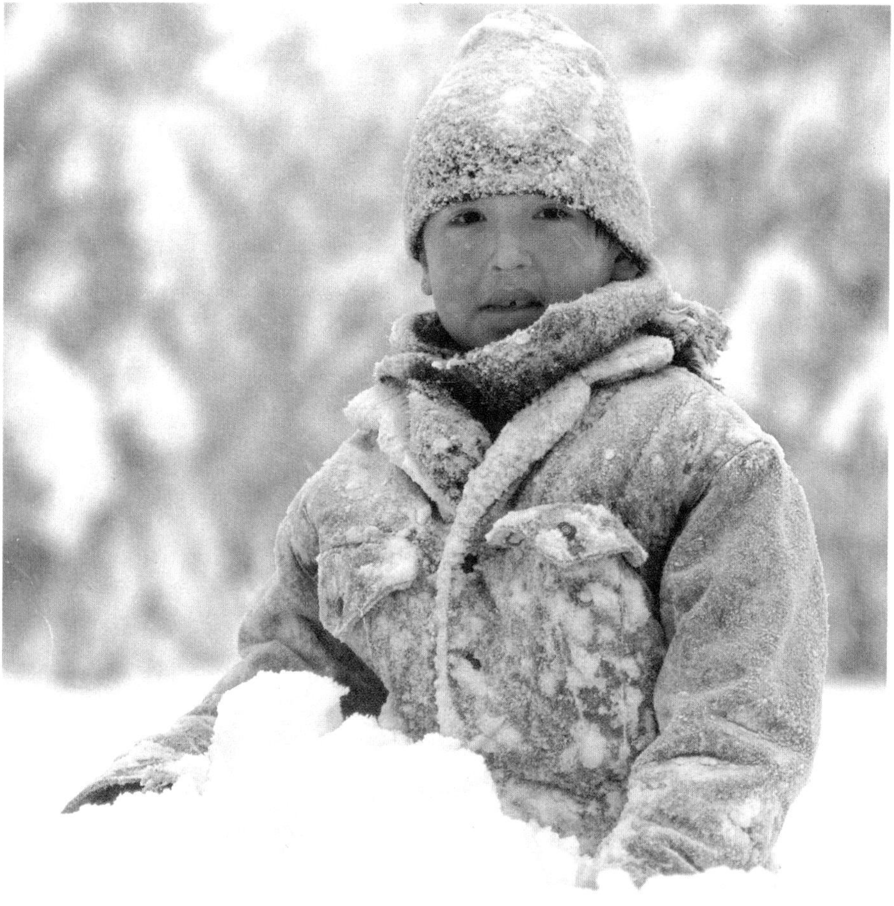

Cold snow all over me.